ADD It Up!

RACHEL FIRST

Consulting Editor, Diane Craig, M.A./Reading Specialist

Sandcastle

An Imprint of Abdo Publishing
abdopublishing.com

abdopublishing.com

Published by Abdo Publishing, a division of ABDO, PO Box 398166, Minneapolis, Minnesota 55439. Copyright © 2016 by Abdo Consulting Group, Inc. International copyrights reserved in all countries. No part of this book may be reproduced in any form without written permission from the publisher. SandCastle™ is a trademark and logo of Abdo Publishing.

Printed in the United States of America, North Mankato, Minnesota

102015
012016

THIS BOOK CONTAINS
RECYCLED MATERIALS

Editor: Liz Salzmann
Content Developer: Nancy Tuminelly
Cover and Interior Design and Production: Mighty Media, Inc.
Photo Credits: Shutterstock

Library of Congress Cataloging-in-Publication Data

First, Rachel, author.
 Add it up! : fun with addition / Rachel First ; consulting editor, Diane Craig, M.A./reading specialist.
    pages cm. -- (Math beginnings)
 ISBN 978-1-62403-932-4
1. Addition--Juvenile literature. 2. Arithmetic--Juvenile literature. I. Title.
 QA115.F554 2016
 513.2'11--dc23
                    2015020613

SandCastle™ Level: Transitional

SandCastle™ books are created by a team of professional educators, reading specialists, and content developers around five essential components—phonemic awareness, phonics, vocabulary, text comprehension, and fluency—to assist young readers as they develop reading skills and strategies and increase their general knowledge. All books are written, reviewed, and leveled for guided reading, early reading intervention, and Accelerated Reader™ programs for use in shared, guided, and independent reading and writing activities to support a balanced approach to literacy instruction. The SandCastle™ series has four levels that correspond to early literacy development. The levels are provided to help teachers and parents select appropriate books for young readers.

EMERGING · BEGINNING · **TRANSITIONAL** · FLUENT

Contents

ADDITION Mission

Addition is a kind of math.

$$2 + 2 = 4$$

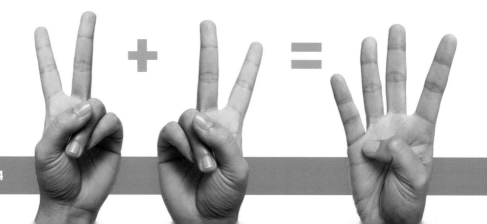

It tells you how much there is.

3 + 2 = 5

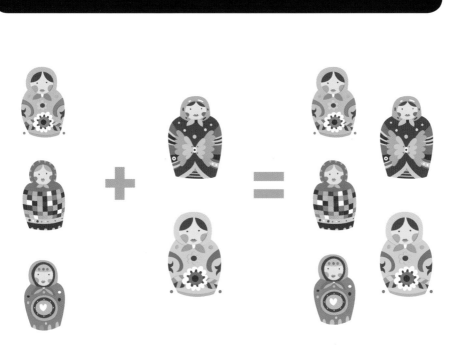

Addition is fun and easy.

Get out four vases.

Then get out three more vases.

Count how many vases there are.

That's addition!

PLUS Sign

8 + 2

plus sign

Addition problems use the plus sign.

Here is a number sentence. Read it, "Eight plus two **equals** ten."

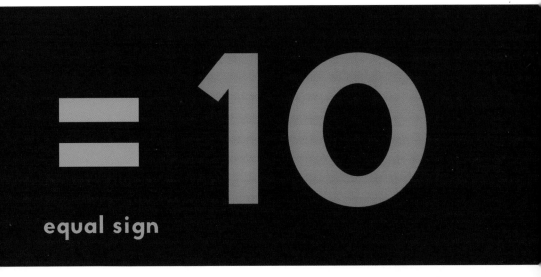

equal sign

A problem can also be **stacked**.
It doesn't have an **equal** sign.
It has a line instead. The
answer goes under the line.

$$3$$
$$+5$$
$$\overline{}$$
$$8$$

Bree likes to add. She has three
problems to do.

How many of Bree's problems can you do? Write down the answers.

What's the SUM?

The answer to an addition problem is called the *sum*.

Sean adds 2 plus 2.
The sum is 4.

WORD Problems

Math problems can be written with words.

Two kids are swimming.

Six more kids jump in the pool.
How many kids are in the pool?

Number LINES

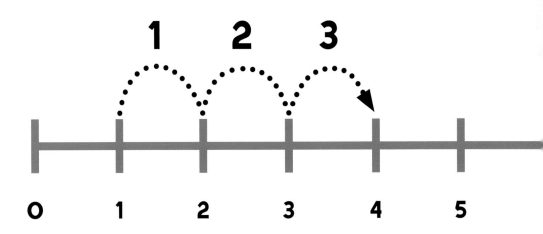

A number line is just that. It's a line with numbers on it. It can help you do **math**.

Move to the right to add. What is 1 + 3?

Put your finger on the 1. Move three numbers to the right. The answer is 4!

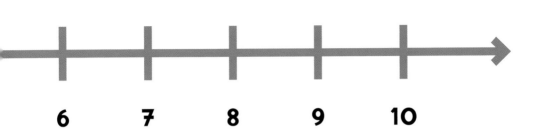

6   7   8   9   10

Number lines can help with word problems.

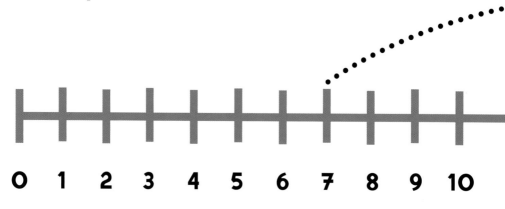

0 1 2 3 4 5 6 7 8 9 10

Jake has seven books. Eva has nine books. How many do they have together?

9

11	12	13	14	15	16	17	18	19	20

Use the number line to find out!

PRACTICE

Draw twelve squares. Write a number in each square. Number them 1 through 12.

Find two small objects. Try beanbags or blocks. Toss the objects onto the squares. What numbers did they land on? Add them together!

$$3 + 6 = 9$$

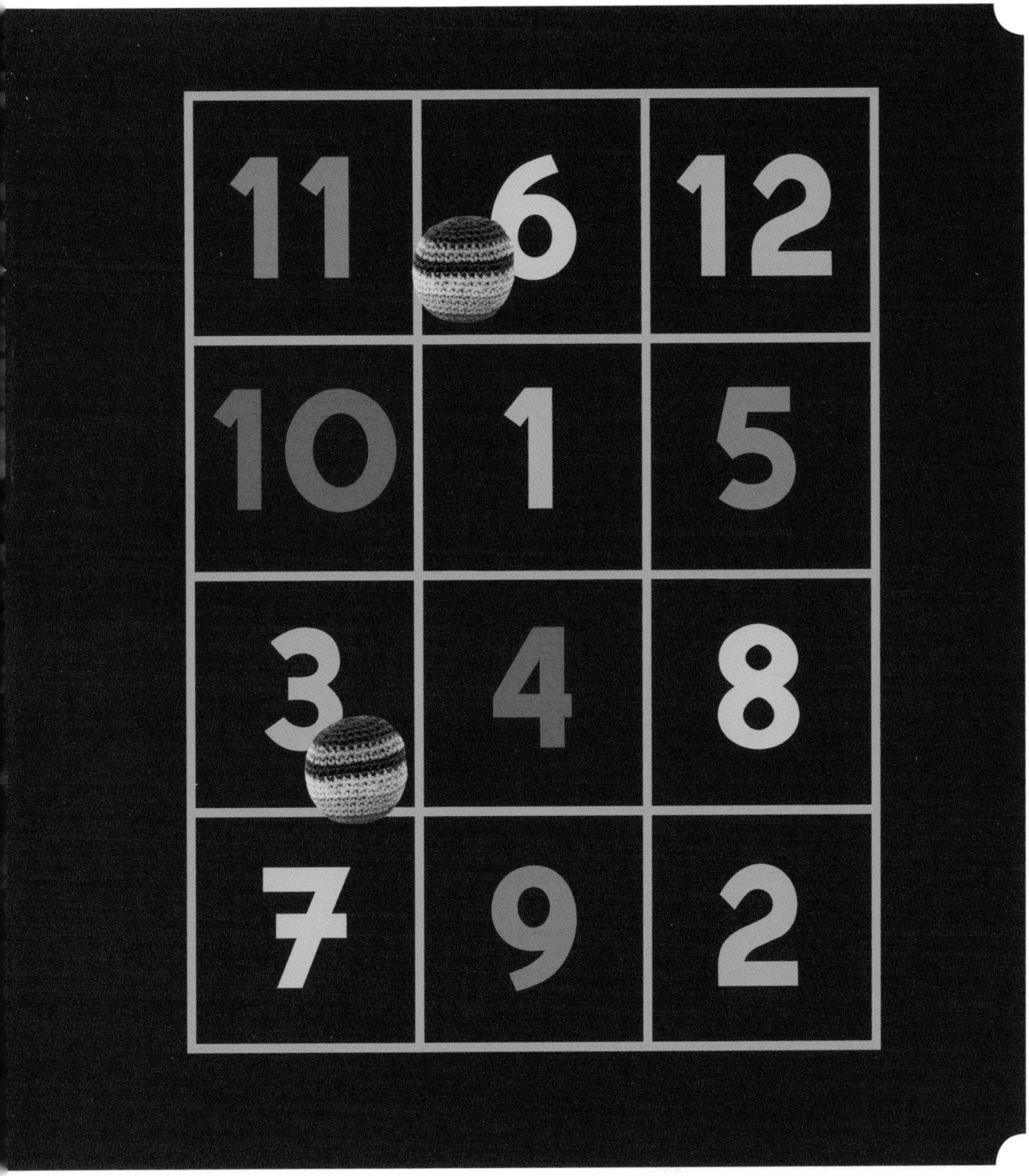
11
6
12
10
1
5
3
4
8
7
9
2

Glossary

BEANBAG – a small bag filled with dry beans that is used in games.

EQUAL – having exactly the same size or amount.

MATH – short for mathematics. The study of numbers and shapes and how they work together.

STACK – to put things on top of each other.